this

little 🌳 ORCHARD

book belongs to

For Dani and Paul Karis

ORCHARD BOOKS
338 Euston Road, London NW1 3BH
*Orchard Books Australia*
Level 17/207 Kent Street, Sydney, NSW 2000
First published in 2001 by Orchard Books
This edition published in 2003
978 1 84362 220 8
Illustrations © Penny Dann 2001
The right of Penny Dann to be identified as
the illustrator of this work has been asserted by her
in accordance with the Copyright, Design and Patents Act, 1988.
A CIP catalogue record for this book is available from the British Library.
1 3 5 7 9 10 8 6 4 2
Printed in China
Orchard Books is a division of Hachette Children's Books,
an Hachette Livre UK company.

# Row, row, row your boat

## Penny Dann

little 🌳 ORCHARD

Row, row, row your boat,

Gently down the stream;

Merrily, merrily, merrily, merrily

Life is but a dream.

Row, row, row your boat,

Gently out to sea;

BACK

Merrily, merrily, merrily, merrily

Then come back with me.

Row, row, row your boat,

Gently on the tide,

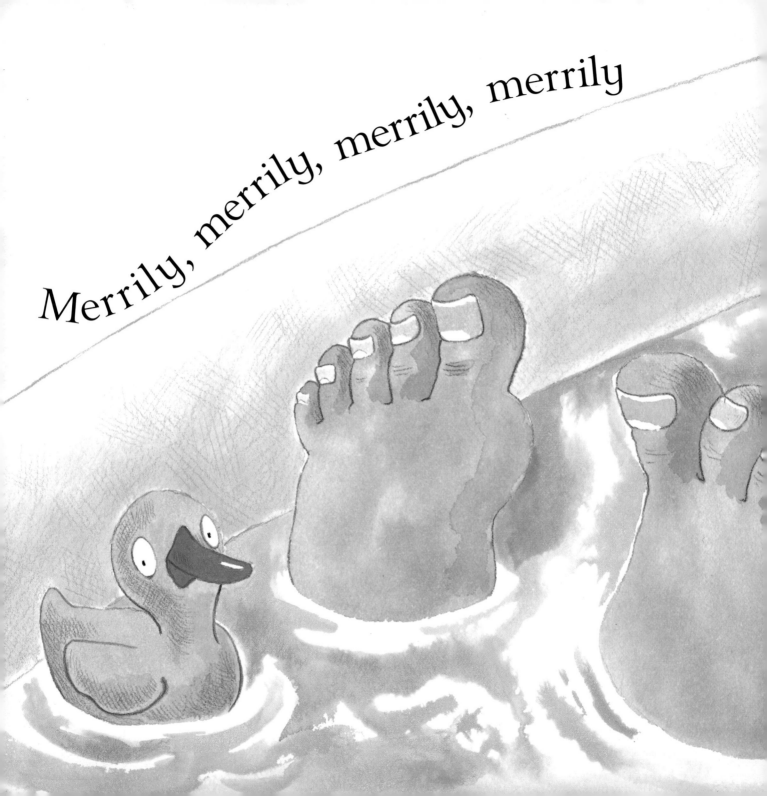

Merrily, merrily, merrily, merrily

To the other side.

Row, row, row your boat,

Gently back to shore;

Merrily, merrily, merrily, merrily

Home for tea at four.